The Mirage
of Separation

THE MIRAGE *OF* SEPARATION

Billy Doyle

NON-DUALITY PRESS

First published March 2008 by Non-Duality Press

Typeset in Dante 12/16 & Syntax 11/16

Cover image: Landscape by Sesshu Toyo, Tokyo National Museum

Non-Duality Press, Salisbury, SP2 8JP
United Kingdom.

ISBN 978-0-9558290-0-0

www.non-dualitybooks.com

"When you step back from stressing the parts, when the mind becomes still, the rose comes to you, unfolds in you in all her glory.

The perfume invades you completely. The rose is you. You are one."

Jean Klein

Introduction

These writings come from a non-dualistic perspective. Our focus is on the nature of our real identity. Until we come to know it, we are lost in a world of ignorance.

Our basic mistake, and from which all other mistakes arise, is to identify ourselves with an object: the body-mind.

In doing so we lose sight of our true nature, consciousness, pure awareness, taking ourselves to be an expression of life, rather than life itself. Thereby we become engrossed in the world of a personalised I; it is this pseudo-I that usurps our real identity.

This I-image, the ego, is no more than a collection of shifting ideas and experiences, with no independent reality. In taking ourselves to be a separate entity we have come adrift from our homeground, and inevitably fear and desire arise. In compensation we pursue happiness and security and try to escape pain and sorrow.

It is only when we understand the illusionary nature of this projection that we become open to our real nature, that which is beyond the mind.

The Self is not something new to be attained, for it ever is; it has only to be recognized.

However we can never know the Self as we would an object, for it is the ultimate knower, neither perceivable, nor conceivable; we can only be it. Its nature is self-luminous.

Billy Doyle
January 2008

Index of first lines

The Mirage of Separation

there was life

then there was life
and somebody living life

then there was life
but nobody living life

then there was life

can I live with the question
never touching it
waiting for the sun to rise
not anticipating the colours
living in this not-knowing
waiting for the inhalation
dissolving with the exhalation
letting the question take its form
letting the answer say what it must

the great understanding
is that you can never understand

the great relief of seeing
no matter how hard I try
I can never understand
I have to leave it to it
that is the understanding

the mind can never take you
to the understanding
but the heart already knows

the fool says
I have understood
but when understanding takes place
there is no one left to say
I have understood

in truth there is
nothing to understand
and there is nobody
to understand it

time is not
where is time when you're not thinking
or in deep sleep
the past, memory, is just a present thought
the future, also a present thought
the present moment, illusive
the instant you try to grasp it, it's gone
there's only the timeless present
the eternal now

you say the journey needs time
but who needs time
inventing time is itself the problem
be free of time and its inventor
rest in the eternal
where time does not encroach

we're invited to sit at the king's table
and worried whether we will eat today
we stand in front of the divine
and talk of the power we experienced at a shrine
we stand in the divine
and discuss how we can find it
we are the very Self
and ask what practice to do to attain it
what comedy do we have here

on hearing the fish in the water
was thirsty, Kabir laughed

if the nightingale asks me for instruction
how to sing, what am I to say

if I visit you in your home
and you tell me you're not there
how am I to believe you

if the Self says it does not know the Self
what deceit is this
the Self cannot be other than the Self
even if it tries to masquerade as the fool

the sunlight cannot penetrate through
the thick foliage of the jungle
reality cannot penetrate the
thick layers of our defence
let go your resistance
drop your shoulders
and let yourself breathe
put away your armour
and give the light just a chance

to see the orchid
you need to get off the express train
simplify your life
stop day-dreaming
take a retreat from the I-concept
and the paraphernalia
of trying to be somebody
then see what's in front of your eyes

Proprietor: Can I help you?

Customer: What can I get here?

Proprietor: There is nothing to get,
but tell me what you are looking for.

Customer: Peace, happiness.

Proprietor: There are no promises here,
we have no carrots and no sugar lumps.

Customer: So what's the deal?

Proprietor: You have to give everything
and expect nothing.
Are you still interested?

Customer: That's why I've come, the
enticements of the world have proved
hollow.
But what must I pay?

Proprietor: You have to pay with your dreams,
fantasies, images, every vanity,
your past, your future, and every
last cent.

Customer: It sounds very reasonable, but do
I not get to keep anything?

Proprietor: If you still want to keep
something you've come
to the wrong establishment.
These are our strict regulations.

Customer: So what will be left?

Proprietor: Why do you ask me such a question?
Are you not finished with the toys
of the phenomenal world? All that
is unreal will be taken away from you.
What remains you'll have to wait
and see.

But perhaps you should go to the
establishment down the road; they have
a three-year course with a recognised
certificate at the end.

Customer: No, no, I have a drawer full.
But could I think about it and come
back tomorrow?

Proprietor: We don't do tomorrows.
There is no time.
There is only now.

the ego seems to take on
a life of its own
and like the devil
likes to play tricks
what to do with this slippery customer
who craves attention
best ignore it
and enjoy your cup of tea

the little I that has taken
up residence inside the head
likes to appropriate everything for itself
only seeing from its blinkered standpoint
claiming to be the doer and thinker
the enjoyer and sufferer
only in the clear light of day
is it seen for what it is
the usurper of the Self
and vanquished to dust

what you really desire is me
you may think it is that new car
but what you really desire is me
you may think it is that other woman
but what you really desire is me
you may play fast and loose
but I know what you really want is me
one day when you've had your fun
you'll just have to admit it
what you really desire is me

desire is a black hole
impossible to fill
nothing in space and time
can satiate its appetite
it devours everything
and still seeks for more
only that beyond space and time
fulfills its longing
and leaves it desireless

when you've gone to the
four corners of the earth
searched under every stone
had lovers throughout the seven seas
explored the eleven dimensions
spoken to all the wise beings
it's time to come home
and sit by your own fire
and see what you've never seen
just waiting for you

bring back your centre of gravity
scattered over the four winds
enticed by every fickle
promise of the world
and let it embed itself
in the only reality

why do we impose
form on the formless

make words of that
which is silence

why localize that
which is non-localized

why reduce to a little me
that which is the vastness

why capture the bird that
soars in the skies
and enclose it in a cage

when you take yourself
to be with form
you will see the other
also with form
and project deities possessing form
when you have understood
you are formless
what "other" can there be
and "who" is there to see "them"

when you use the word I
let it be free of all images
let it be free of I am this, I am that
when you use the word I
let it be free of yesterday and tomorrow
let it reside in timelessness
let it resonate in space
without any border
without any centre
let all the small 'I's dissolve back into it
do not try to grasp or touch it with the mind
for it is always beyond, and yet closer
this I, you can only be

pure subjectivity
non-differentiation
don't clutter beauty
with personal pronouns

form is an expression of the formless
time is an expression of the timeless
words are an expression of the wordless
all that is perceived
is within the perceiver
so why emphasise the outer
forgetting the inner

let form come back to the formless
let time come back to the timeless
let words come back to the wordless
let the perception come back
to the perceiving
let all rest
in its homeground

after eliminating each layer
that you are not
body, senses, mind
and arriving at nothing
don't stop there, proceed
and eliminate the nothing

in the Self
there is neither Arab or Jew
black or white
Hutu or Tutsi
high caste or low caste
male or female
remove the coat of paint
and only consciousness is revealed
the Self only sees the Self

the scent of the rose
is not in the flower
it is in you

the sound of the Beethoven quartet
is not in the instruments
it is in you

the taste of the mango
is not in your mouth
it is in you

the poem
is not on the page
it is in you

the sunset
is not in the sky
it is in you

meditation
a practice no one can practise
abandoning all hope
free of a doer
no intention or goal
accepting and surrendering
all that arises
going nowhere
for where would one go
and who is there to go
giving all to the moment
the moment that cannot be thought
not knowing, not knowing, not knowing

there is not
when the clay pot breaks
where is the space inside and outside
where is the you and the me
the here and there
the rising and the setting
the day and the night
the pure and the impure
there is not

volition is the devil
makes you think you can attain
but the ultimate is not
to be attained
all volition ensnares you
deeper into the black pit of illusion
thinking you've achieved something

your compassion for the world is admirable
but where is the compassion for the Self
smothered beneath a mountain of concepts
it can barely breathe
see through the illusion
of being a separate entity
of being I am this, I am that
and let the Self breathe forth

fighting the ego is a great battle
that monster from the underworld
every minute you must be vigilant
and ready to take up sword
but does the creature really exist
have the sightings been verified
are they any more than your thoughts
are you not wrestling with a phantom
where is the ego
when you're not inventing it

the ego is as sticky as glue
all the debris collects round it
producing karmic layering
burying you deep in your individuality
but to the Self nothing can cling
being nothing, insults pass unregistered
praise, adulation likewise
nothing invades sacred space
for there is nothing outside
and nothing to defend

the winds of thought
puff up the sails of the ego
and blow you hither and thither
from crest to trough
from pleasure to pain
but if you just observe
these thoughts with disinterest
they will subside
and the sails of the ego
will go slack
and you will be
one with the ocean

not the faintest whiff of objectivity
not a speck of its corrosive dust
no-thing to touch or see
and no-body touching or seeing
where past and future
have no echo
no borders, only I

Maybe you know this story:

There was once a fish called Agonda
that heard of this marvellous thing called water.
It went on a long search from ocean to ocean
asking many a wise fish where water was to be
found. After years of fruitless journeys and much
misleading advice, Agonda was discussing her
plight with a rather ordinary-looking fish she met
by some rocks. It told Agonda:
"The water is all around you."
Agonda was astonished, and laughing at herself
felt overjoyed.

> *We seek happiness thinking it must be*
> *something outside us to be acquired. We*
> *look in every direction until we realise it is*
> *not outside, but our real nature, nearer than*
> *the nearest, we have always been at home.*

There was once a king called Alexi, who on
waking one morning after a strange dream
found his wife missing. He sent his courtiers
throughout his kingdom in search of her.
But after a year had passed and no success
he was almost suicidal. Then one morning
on waking he remembered he had never been
married.

*Our misery is created by the illusion we lack
something. When we wake up in our real
nature we realise nothing was ever missing.*

you know the world around you
you know your house
you know your body, your thoughts,
emotions, your personality
but who is this knower
you can never know the knower
it is not an object to be known
it is the eternal background
the silence
that which you are

it is ignorance to know
the diversity of the whole world
and never to have asked
who is the knower

the tree you can touch
the grass you can feel
the Self you cannot touch it

the sunset you can see
you can see the autumn leaves
the Self is never seen

you can hear the flute
and the child laughing
you will not hear the Self

the orange blossom has a fragrance
so does the freshly cut grass
the Self is without any fragrance

there is no doubting
the taste of the mango
or the taste of honey
but you will not taste the Self

you can think about your beloved
or the nature of time
but you can never think of the Self
it lies beyond the contamination
of the mind
ever present

don't try to be aware
for you are already awareness
just note you lose yourself in thought

don't try to be silent
for you are already silence
just note the lack of silence

don't try to be at peace
for you are already peace
just note the lack of peace

it's nonsense trying to be
what you already are
awareness, silence, peace
the rose does not try to be a rose

it's before you see
it's before you hear
it's before you think
how can you doubt it
it's nearer than the nearest

it needs no eyes to see it
it needs no ears to hear it
it needs no mind to think it

the concept is an abstraction
keeps us in the fog of the mind
reinforcing the past
in pure perception we're closer
to ourselves, to reality
simply seeing, hearing, feeling
tasting, smelling
with no space for an
interfering I

the ego is a prison
trying to escape
only reinforces the walls
you can change the decor
but still you're in chains
until the occupant is seen
    for what he is
      pure illusion
then where is the prisoner
and where is the prison

the ego is like the devil
they can only exist in the
darkness of the mind
when the light shines
they're out the back door
too embarrassed to show their faces

the sky is deep blue
jasmine fills the air
enough of all these questions
all these queries why
time to jump into life's stream
and unencumbered
enjoy the beauty there

the sun shines
it does not choose to shine
the frog jumps
it does not choose to jump
love flows
it does not choose to flow

don't stoke up the fire
with more grandiose illusions

don't place more wood
of day-dreaming to enflame

ignore the sparks
from the dying embers
telling yesterday's tales

let the fire burn itself out
and feel the coolness of the ashes

that whole tale of a me
has no credibility
I've peered deep inside
it's quite preposterous
I simply don't believe a word of it any more
as that character struts across the stage
creating endless dramas
he takes himself so seriously
totally identified with his role
but I think it's sheer comedy
as I'm trying not to laugh
too loud, at the door

eternity is in this moment
not the next
in this breath
not the next
in this expression
not some other

discover what is not born
and does not die
discover where there is no bondage
and where there is no liberation
birth, death, bondage, liberation
    mind stuff

why not stand aside
get out of your own way
and let nobody do things for you
drive your car, do the shopping, pay your bills
without your hang-ups
it will do things much better
and without an interfering busybody
life will flow on smoothly
and at the end of the day
nobody sleeps like a baby

if you know whilst dreaming
you're dreaming
what matter if the shadows
of demons cross your wall
if your boat is sinking in the sea
a tiger appears in the undergrowth
you know it's but a dream

if you know you are the Self
what matter if the body becomes ill
your shares are in freefall
your lover takes flight

 you rest untouched
 forever in the Self

don't wait to become perfect
before knowing you are perfect

don't wait to become silent
before knowing you are the silence

don't wait to become enlightened
before knowing you are enlightened

time is not going to take you
to the timeless

why this waiting
it's already happened
it happened before you were born
it's happening each moment
no, not in a parallel universe
but in front of your eyes
behind your eyes
prior to the first thought
now and always

love's look is indiscriminate
it bathes all with the same gaze
no moment is more precious
than the next
no breath more special
than the one before
it does not choose
this or that
its fragrance envelops all
it excludes none
for all is itself

this one sees and hears only itself
celebrating forever only itself
only itself does it love
it leaves no room for otherness
and takes possession of all that is
there is no escape from this one
you may dream yourself separate
but the dream is not apart from the one

at the moment of death
there's a saying goodbye
to all that was held dear

a closing of eyes
to all that was possessed

a laying aside
of body and mind

a falling back of the wave
into the ocean

a surrender of all
that we are not

but why postpone
this moment

there is no security in a me
it's always crumbling at the edges
in constant need of repair
fear is the constant companion
the only security is the
dissolution of the me
silence
is beyond security
and insecurity

here is the invitation
it's always beckoning
it's in the air
in the birdsong
when you dive into the ocean
when you're lost in the rhythms
of the gypsy music
when you are taken
by the eyes of another
this enticing invitation
    death

death, go deep within
into the darkness
give yourself to death
let your fire burn it to ashes

there is no path to take you
    any closer to me
there is no path to take you
    any further away
    how could there be
    I abide in the Heart

sit in the Self
inhale in the Self
exhale in the Self
let the attention
rest in the Self

gold is shaped into many ornaments
yet is it not all just gold

waves form a myriad of shapes and sizes
yet they are all just water

the canvas evokes a beautiful landscape
yet it is just a mixture of paint

the film on the screen conjures up a whole story
yet it is just the play of light

the world is full of tragedies and triumphs
yet it is just the play of consciousness

when you are one of the branches of the tree
every breeze shakes you
every storm buffets you this way and that
you fear for your life
but when you become the trunk
you stay unmoved in the storm
you may feel the pull of the branches
but you are in stillness

when you are a wave in the ocean
every wind and current pushes and drags
sometimes shattering you
but when you are the depth of the ocean
what are a few gusts on the surface

you cannot become other than you are
better to take on trust from the beginning
the words of the sage
that all is gold
otherwise you may spend lifetimes
trying to convert brass into gold
a labour doomed to failure

that which is nameless and formless
knows no dust
trying to polish it
is like trying to polish the universe
perhaps you're wasting your time

in the direct approach
the journey is negated before it begins
after all a journey would allow
you to indulge in time and space
and what would you be without
the additions of time and space

in the direct approach
there's no time for self-improvement
and the illusions it gives you
you are up against a wall
there's no escape
to see reality, here, now

for the divine to enter
you need to clean up your own house
open up the windows
sweep away the cobwebs
vacuum each room
clear out your basement
and chase away the ghosts
lurking in the attic
after the dust has settled
you might find
your visitor already at home

alternatively, if you're short of time
see that there is no dust
you don't have a home
there is no visitor
and there is no you

People spend a lifetime trying to control the mind, but to what purpose? The controller with its agenda of controlling only reinforces the centre, the I-image, that which it is trying to free itself from.

It betrays a deep distrust of life. The controller is thought, the weaver of division. Controlling the mind is setting a thief to catch a thief. It is dealing with the symptoms and not the cause. A controlled mind confined within walls is rigid, dead to the spontaneity of life. Only in understanding the nature of thought, and the mind seeing its own limits, does quietness descend. Silence is not of the mind, but 'behind' the mind, ever still.

there are many techniques
      to stop thoughts
you can focus on the third eye
      recite mantras
      count each breath
until you realise nobody's thinking
the thinker is itself just a thought

I keep myself veiled
only revealing myself to the innocent
I keep myself hidden
only to be found
by those willing to make the search
my price is not insubstantial
your life is my fee
in this game of hide and seek
the world is my reflection
the shadow will take you
to the source
the wave has the taste
of the sea
I'm not so far away
as you imagine

I'm there between each breath
but you don't see me

I'm there between each thought
but you ignore me

I'm there when you've attained
your desire
but you don't acknowledge me

I'm there in your heart
but you don't feel my beat

I'm always in front of your eyes
but you don't recognize me

don't take the in-breath
let it come to you

don't grasp the flower with your eyes
let it reveal itself to you

don't run after truth
let it find you

don't try to absorb the ultimate
let the ultimate absorb you

though it's remarkably close
try as you may
you can never catch
the divine in your net
any more than you can scoop out
the ocean with a ladle
you can't even approach the divine
for distance there is not
but when the mirage of separation dissolves
it's the divine that has
scooped you up in its net

sweep out the last dust of volition
hiding in the recesses
rid yourself of the volition
trapped in your jaw
extricate the volition still
polluting your eyes
let go the volition cramping
your hands
and give yourself to the
will of the divine

there comes a time
when you have to let go
all the words
all the teaching
and trust the infinite

karma is for him who
takes himself to be an individual
for him who believes he is subject
to time and space
for him who has the notion he was born

but in the Self, crystal clear
what can karma mean
there's not even a speck of dust
and never has been

remove everything
you know about yourself
everything objective
it is not you
only decoration
be with what remains

in the midst of a chaotic world
is there not that which is always at peace

in the midst of ceaseless change
is there not that which is changeless

beyond all the self images
is there not the purest of the pure

perhaps in reality
there is perfection right now

what is there before the thought
and after the thought
it is not nothing, but presence, consciousness

what is there before the in-breath
and after the out-breath
it is not nothing, but presence, consciousness

what is there before you see the blackbird
and after you see the blackbird
it is not nothing, but presence, consciousness

why do we lose ourselves in the ephemeral
and forget the eternal background

oceans
horizon beyond horizon
infinite space
mind without reference
free of all frontiers
    there
take your abode

no hold
no compass
no latitude or longitude
no reason why
just the dance of the ocean
the great tide
flows where it will

forest fires cannot burn it

a tsunami cannot cover it

all the concrete in China

will not compress it

a hurricane cannot blow it a centimetre

    death and birth

    do not sway it

the mind can never encompass it

the temple of nothingness
    is not for visiting only
    on a Friday or a Sunday
the god of nothingness you cannot
reduce to a form and worship
the boat of nothingness
is not going to take you anywhere
    you are not already

when we reach the end of our lives
and look back, we may wonder
where did it all go
we were seldom really there
present to the moment
we were always somewhere else
escaping, fixed on some object
seeking after another mirage
running away from ourselves

all that is acquired
will be lost

all that is new
will become old

all that which was born
will die

all that which was learnt
will be forgotten

seek out only the Real
the ever present

what is this me
a bundle of yesterday's memories
a mass of resistance to what is
a non-acceptance of the moment
a bodily contraction from the
embrace of now
a wanting to be somewhere else
dreaming of a more perfect time
a refusal of the gift in our hands

but no need to resist this me
invite it home, humour it
and when loved
can it resist any more

not a journey for the faint-hearted
not to be taken lightly
it's going to take heart and mind
you have to be on fire with your question
no room for self-deceit
only a ruthless honesty will suffice
no time to indulge in day-dreaming
no more detours
to dismantle yourself completely
not a fragment left
to live without yesterdays
without a persona
are you willing to be nobody

it is this, here, now
but the mind would prefer
an encyclopaedia about it
than to be with the simplicity
of this message
we don't want to hear this
we would prefer a journey
with the prospect of miraculous
experiences along the way
and to live forever in hope
than to be with this, here, now

have you noticed
nothing ever really happens
true, there's a light show
sound show, thought show
and all that
but the screen
has it ever changed
you may cross continents
but presence is simply presence

when there is a glimpse
of our true nature
we become orientated
no longer scattered
here and there
there's simplicity
all the iron filings
are drawn back to the core
only one question
only one teacher
only one

in the moment there is no space
for the past
in the moment there is no space
for the future
in the moment there is no space
for being a me and a you
in the moment
there's nothing lacking

the dark muddy river
is enclosed in concrete underground
the soul is smothered beneath
the comfort of body and mind

sometimes it tries to speak to us
in the dark of the night
but is forgotten by morning
with the coming of light

the stars are all but obliterated
in our neon life
who bothers to remember the soul
though it's all that we've got

the greatest joy is to be
free of the greatest burden, yourself
that ton of bricks we carry
with its labyrinth of tunnels
corridors and lines of defence
that we spend our life
crawling round like automatons
oblivious to the joy
that is the Self

silence, stillness
for the mind, boring, an enigma
like a dark cave
but explore it
go deeper into the darkness
embrace it
glimpses of light flicker
until there's only light

nothing has ever been held back
emptiness has always been fullness
love has never kept anything for itself
nothing is missing
the well is always overflowing
only in the dream
is there a lack

after a lifetime
of struggling to know
the surprise of finding home
in not-knowing
like a return to childhood
without the child
in this not-knowing
nothing remains to be known

knowledge brings innocence
the sage is as a child
happy for no reason
his actions seem purposeless
the future and its strategies
are of no concern
he is guileless
for what does he lack
his smile melts your defences

it is born and then dies
it is not I
one day it is happy, another day sad
it is not I
it is accepted and adored
then rejected and despised
it is not I
it feels rich and then
complains of being poor
it is not I
it is in health and then sickness
it is not I

without a blemish
what care I about such matters
I am no-body, no-thing
untouchable
beyond all opposites

who am I
you may look under every stone
search every nook and cranny
but you won't find very much
just a collection of phantoms
look deeper, deeper
these disappear
leaving only transparency and space

here, if there can be a here
as at the birth of time
all is held in its potentiality
and yes, too, the expression
spread out across an infinity
and yet in all this
not a wave of a mine or a yours
in this borderless expanse

be detached from the world

and be detached from
him who would be detached

and be detached
from detachment

stack the funeral pyre high
for the cremation of the me
to burn to ash the illusion
the sacred wood is knowledge
there is nothing to obtain
all progress belongs to an object
all directions are the wrong directions
dreams are but dreams
don't mourn the passing
it was its deepest wish
it had no more reality
than the wafting smoke

joy needs no cause or excuse
any more than the sun
needs a reason to shine
it is our essence
that's why we all seek it
but it is us that pull the blinds
when it does visit unexpectedly
do not look for a reason
we were simply open
and not pulling the blinds

what you are needs no embellishment
there is no place to hang earrings
there is no face to paint
nothing needs to be added or subtracted
gilding this lily only buries it
its joy is its nakedness
free of man and woman, you and me
free of the drapery
of high office or low office
it needs no formulation
it shines of itself

you would like to give up
all you are not
the insanity of individuality
piece by piece
but there's always another
subtlety lurking below
the real giving up
is seeing that there
is nobody to give up anything

wisdom is understanding
the nature of subject and object
that I am the ultimate subject
and the body, senses and mind
and hence the world
are my objects
and then to go one step further
and see the apparent subject
and the apparent object
are one

there is only this

there is no other shore
but this shore

there is no other consciousness
but this consciousness

there is no other enlightenment
but this enlightenment

there is no other to become
but what I am

one step away
and I'm already lost

there is only this

what you are is non-conceptual
it is prior to the conceptual
so you cannot possibly think it
the mind is not the appropriate tool
it is clarity itself
and nothing you can do
or say about it
try as you may

the moon has no light of its own
it borrows its light
from the sun
the body-mind has no light
of its own
it is borrowed from consciousness
you are the light
that illuminates all that is

peace is not the peace
you feel at the end of the day

silence is not the silence
when the noise stops, or a thought ceases

beauty is not
the beauty in the sunset

peace, silence, beauty
have never come into being
and have never departed
nothing can destroy
for they are not of time

thoughts come and go
in the vastness
feelings come and go
in the vastness
bird song comes and goes
in the vastness
all are but ripples
in the vastness

do not go to the temple
leave not your home

do not climb the holy mountain
leave not your home

do not wander along
the path to some nirvana
leave not your home

enough of all this acquiring and seeking
leave not your home

for the seeker is the sought
leave not your home

that which you seek
is not to be found
it is much too close to touch
much too close to see
it is the touching
it is the seeing
there are not two
or some other
the necklace you thought was missing
is still around your neck

the usurper of the Self
would like to prolong its reign
even beyond the grave
so for its comfort
and for the continuation
of the story of a me
it consoles itself with reincarnation
but if we really lived the moment
would we be imagining
some other body, some other time
or even tomorrow

it's but name and form
chaff in the wind
why run after the dust
when you stand on the bedrock
it's but name and form
it dies with the blink of an eye
the plaything of time and space
but the continuum
the eternal melody
is beyond all sense

if there is a path to understanding
that path is silence
all arises out of silence
and through silence
we make our journey back
in silence there's no hold for the mind
all fabrication of the me comes to rest
the words of the sage
are bathed in silence
but we have to let their form dissolve
to let them take us from whence they came
no one can possess silence
it possesses all
silence does not come and go
you do not experience silence
it is not an object
it is the experiencing
silence has no opposite
for all is its expression
it is the eternal background
the homeground

Consciousness, there is no looking for, no possibility of experiencing, because you can only experience what is outside yourself, an object, phenomena. It is because you are so deeply anchored, inseparable from consciousness, the noumenon, you cannot experience it, it has no otherness you could experience. Otherwise it would not be consciousness but another object of consciousness. Not for a moment could you stand outside and look back at consciousness. There are not two.

Atmananda Krishna Menon said, 'You feel it without feeling it.' Jean Klein would often say, 'The eye cannot see its own seeing.'

the silence
that is unrecognizable
leaves no footprint in the sand
not a trace of yesterday
yet knows itself
sees all, and is all seen
it leaves no signature
emptiness walks through emptiness
with no memory of itself

a vigil for the Self
long into the night
waiting without expectation
what might I be
no answer was forthcoming
but the question was no more
nothing was missing
the silence was home

follow the language
that has no letters, no words
that nobody can speak
that nobody can hear
listen deeply
be open to it
let it embrace you
it is only this language
that will take you
to the secret garden

Printed in the United States
124388LV00002B/103/P

9 780955 829000